THE JOY OF
DANCING

ACKNOWLEDGEMENTS

Written & compiled by
PEGGY SPENCER MBE

Consultant editor
ANNA McCORQUODALE

Dance steps photographer
HEINZ LAUTENBACHER

Dance steps performed by:
Ballroom
CHRISTOPHER HAWKINS & HAZEL NEWBERRY
Latin
JOHN BYRNES &
JANE LYTTLETON

Professional dance pictures supplied by
CHRISANNE LIMITED
CHOICE LONDON LIMITED
RON SELF

Dance shoes pictures
SUPERDANCE INTERNATIONAL

THE JOY OF
DANCING

Ballroom, Latin and Rock/Jive
for Absolute Beginners of All Ages

PEGGY SPENCER MBE

CARLTON
BOOKS

ADVICE TO THE READER

Before following any exercise advice contained in this book, it is recommended that you consult your doctor if you suffer from any health problems or special conditions, or if you are in any doubt as to its suitablity.

First published in Great Britain in 1997 by Chameleon Books
an imprint of André Deutsch Ltd

This edition published in 2004 by
Carlton Books
20 Mortimer Street
London W1T 3JW

Printed in Italy

A catalogue record for this book is available from the British Library

ISBN 1 84442 547 9

Designed by Anita Ruddell

FOREWORD

As Chairman of the British Dance Council, I am delighted to have been given the opportuninty to contribute to *The Joy of Dancing*. To those who know it, Ballroom and Latin dancing offers a superb experience as entertainment, as a pastime, as a sport, and as an exercise. Beyond that, it is also great fun.

Outside our world of Ballroom and Latin dancing, there are many millions of people who, if they were given the opportunity and the confidence to dip their toes into our world, would find for themselves many opportunities for enjoyment, healthy exercise, an introduction into the sporting side of dancing and, possibly above all, the opportunity to make many, many friends.

While there are many different ways in which people have been introduced to this wonderful pastime, *The Joy of Dancing* offers a straightforward no-nonsense guide to Ballroom and Latin dancing, which should be introduction enough to learn and to inspire inquisitiveness, and give enough confidence to take that deep breath and go to a dancing class. If you have thought of ballroom dancing as the kind of dancing that your Great Grandparents were doing at the turn of the century, remember that they enjoyed it, and so can you.

Dancing itself changes, as it should. New styles and new dances come into being, but the instinct to dance and the enjoyment of it are timeless and enduring. From the Waltz to the Rock/Jive, there are forms of dance that will be exciting to all ages. Peggy Spencer needs to be congratulated for offering you, the reader, that chance – possibly the chance of a lifetime! – to take the first steps on a journey into the wonderful world of dancing. To everyone who wishes to enjoy the pleasure of dancing, music, atmosphere and colour, this book should prove invaluable.

Freddie Boultwood

Former Chairman
British Dance Council

CONTENTS

'HELLO' FROM PEGGY SPENCER

CHAIRMAN OF THE IMPERIAL SOCIETY OF TEACHERS OF DANCING

EAR DANCERS

I have called this book *The Joy of Dancing* and frankly this title sums up my feeling about all forms of social dancing with particular emphasis on Ballroom and Latin American.

Perhaps the most exciting trend of the past few years has been the re-discovery of Ballroom and Latin American by young people all over the world. I can't begin to tell you how much pleasure it gives me to know that in colleges and community centres in Great Britain one of the most popular club activities is dancing. Yes, dancing together with a partner is now acceptable, and it is even more fun to learn some of the steps of the more popular dances which are featured in this book.

I have tried to make the instructions and illustrations as easy as possible to follow, but do remember that practise makes perfect. You will find it is like learning to ride a bike, it will suddenly all click into place and you will experience a sense of movement and style which is tremendously exhilarating.

What is also exhilarating is that across Britain, five million people dance in some form or other every week. Dance schools and classes are attracting people from every walk of life. Dance has no religion, politics, age barrier or culture problems. Dance is for everyone.

Dancing and music have been with us since the beginning of time. People have danced to celebrate joyful occasions, the birth of a baby, a wedding, to ask for rain to make the crops

grow, or to give thanks for it's arrival. Dance has always been a very important part of life all over the world. Look at a baby in it's pram and see the little fingers and toes dancing automatically. The innate feeling of music is there from the very beginning of life.

If you can master the basic steps laid out in this book you will always be able to enjoy wherever there is a celebration or party with music. You will be amazed how being able to dance will boost your confidence and at the same time allow you to make so many new friends. Dancing is about partners and partnerships which are the core of our lives.

So dear readers let me finish by repeating my theme: the joy of dancing. You don't have to be a Fred Astaire or Ginger Rogers to enjoy dancing. Everyone can do it. So push back the furniture, and start learning. As the song says, 'I could have danced all night' Why not!

Happy Dancing.

INTRODUCTION:
HOW TO USE THIS BOOK

*T*HIS BOOK IS ESSENTIALLY A WORKBOOK for social dancers who are absolute beginners, to enable beginners to understand and learn with confidence the first steps of the most frequently used social dances. You will then be ready to dance at social functions, weddings, on a cruise, or on holiday. You will also be ready to attend a dancing school, where you can improve your technique.

This book has been written in language that can be understood by the beginner, and is in no way intended to be a technical book: those studying dancing as a profession have their own technical books. Instead, this book intends to take the fear and mystique out of dancing to make it *fun*. It can be used on its own, following the photographs and the step-by-step instructions, or in conjunction with one or both of my videos: *Ballroom Dancing* and *Latin American Dancing For Absolute Beginners*, available from VCI.

In *The Joy of Dancing* the dances are divided into two categories: Ballroom dances and Latin American dances. The Waltz, Foxtrot, Quickstep and Tango are known as Ballroom dances. Although Rock 'n' Roll is a dance category in its own right, in this book I have included Rock/Jive in the Ballroom dances so that it is in the same category as it is on my *Absolute Beginners* videos. The Cha Cha Cha, Samba, Mambo, Rumba and Merengue are the Latin American dances.

It is important to remember that there are *no set rules* for the order in which the dances

should be learned. It is entirely your choice. One *very* important rule, though, is to learn slowly and think positively. In other words, don't try to do too much too quickly. One idea is to select the two basic steps in the Waltz and work on them not only until your feet are working the correct steps, but also until your knees and body have become relaxed and your legs are moving easily and smoothly. You will then be able to dance well with your partner.

This book is full of valuable information to help the absolute beginner to understand the basic steps of each dance. You will achieve a clear understanding of the correct hold position, poise and the right direction to proceed around the ballroom. The many do's and dont's are essential nuggets of information that will help you become an efficient dancer. There is a section on how to relate dance to keeping fit, suggestions as to what the social dancer might want to wear to dance in, with some special advice on shoes. Throughout, there are tips on ballroom etiquette to help you to have a wonderful time dancing, as well as a list of useful addresses and contacts to help your dancing develop with ease and enjoyment.

Read the following pages carefully before embarking on the step-by-step learning. They will help you understand the language of dance and prepare you for most eventualities. Most importantly, they will also give you the confidence to start learning.

Having absorbed all the general advice, you will be ready to select the dance you wish to study first. If you are practising with a partner, take a Double-hand Hold (see page 121) when walking through the steps. If you are practising alone then use the same hold depending on whether you are leading or following and imagine the position of your partner. Bear in mind that most clubs, dance halls, and hotel ballrooms are usually crowded and correct social hold, leading and directions are essential. Gradually take the correct hold with your partner and practise the steps to music as this will make them become easier and more natural. To dance well means coordinating your feet, body, arms and head with the music. Without music there is no dance. So have patience. And remember: practise makes *almost* perfect.

POISE

Poise is one of the most important parts of learning to dance. Without good poise the correct balance of the body is in doubt. For example, if a man is leaning forward from the waist over his partner, he puts her in a most uncomfortable position. If the lady is clinging on to the man with her left hand holding his right hand in a tight grip, this is equally as uncomfortable for her partner.

★ Stand normally with the shoulders down and the head over the backbone.
★ Keep the body relaxed and flexible, but with steady and controlled tension.
★ Practise walking forward and back just brushing your ankles against each other to achieve control and balance when you are moving.

Once you have fully mastered the walks forward and back in a comfortable and balanced way, you will have achieved fairly good poise.

A FEW INITIAL POINTS

★ You don't need to learn the dances in any special order. Select the dance you wish to concentrate on first and have the correct music ready.
★ Always study the direction in which the dance will progress around the Ballroom very carefully.
★ Be sure to only analyse the poise and then the basic action, or the basic step of the dance at first.
★ Concentrate on relaxing your knees, and relaxing your hips so that you can respond to the music. If your body is tight and tense it will not react to the music.
★ Work hard on achieving the first basic steps before attempting any kind of variation. At most social functions it is possible (and necessary) to dance only the basic steps, so it can be a waste of time to learn lots of variations.
★ Courtesy dictates that variations should not be tried on a new partner.
★ Bear in mind that foot positions alone do not make the dance. Combine good foot position with a flexible body and a musical frame of mind.
★ The term "Small Step" is of major importance. For social dancing most dances are more enjoyable, and much easier to lead, if the steps are kept very small. The dance will then become elegant, balanced, and controllable.
★ Although you might practise the steps in an empty room, remember that this will not be the scene when you go to a party or dance. In the same way as, if you learn how to drive a car on an empty road, you will still have to learn how to drive that car in traffic, you have to learn to guide and steer your partner in and out of other dancers without causing collisions, and still keep the direction of the dance correct. To do this the man must make sure that he knows his steps sufficiently well.
★ Always study the poise and the hold of each dance.

THE HOLD

In the normal hold, the lady's head must be turned slightly to her left, in other words, looking over the man's right shoulder. Her head should not be turned into a forward-looking direction, except when Promenade figures (see page 121) are danced. This is perhaps the lady's most common fault, but when it comes to direction, the lady must rely on her partner, and she must remain sensitive to his lead. She should remain passive in relationship to the man so that she is not pulling him off balance.

★ This can be practised by doing a continuous number of swings and folds, until the position becomes quite natural.

HOW TO PRACTISE

Learning the best way to practise is very important, and the following tips also apply if you are learning from the videos.

★ Find a spot where you have enough room to practise the dance of your choice over and over again, until the steps become very familiar and you don't have to think too hard.

★ If you are practising with a partner, it is a good idea to use the practice hold, that is, the Double-hand Hold (see page 121).

★ Work out the steps together so that the lady understands the man's lead and the man understands how to lead his lady. He needs to be able to communicate to his partner which foot he is going to use, and whether he is going forward or backwards or sideways.

★ Practise your steps to the music and carefully coordinate any turns that you may be attempting, always thinking of the correct directions.

★ Don't underestimate the amount of practise necessary to be able to dance freely and easily. Eventually you will be able to chat with your partner without having to think about the steps all the time.

WARM-UP TIPS

Any physical activity requires the body to be ready. You'll get rewarding results if you take a few minutes to warm up. The following are a few warm-up tips. Make sure that every action is gentle and performed with care.

Neck Release Stretch your neck gently upwards to release tension, and then turn your head slowly to the right and then to the left. While doing this try to feel tall. This will help you achieve a good poise.

Shoulders Roll each shoulder in a half- circular motion and then lift both shoulders up and down to achieve a total relaxed feeling. Relaxed and dropped shoulders are essential for good dancing.

Hips Holding on to a wall or a chair, free the hip joints by gently swinging each leg forward and back – keeping the foot slightly off the floor. Dancing requires the hip joints to move softly and freely.

Knees Loosen knee joints by lifting each knee in turn. This will help the fluid to circulate around the knee joints ready for dancing.

Ankles Extend your foot slightly and circle the ankle, first to the right and then to the left. Work on each ankle alternately.

Toes Dancing requires light movements with the feet. Rise on to the toes and gently lower your weight into whole foot. This is an important exercise. It gives the whole foot a chance to work from the heel to the ball of the foot to the toes and then from the toes to the ball of the foot to the whole foot.

Hands and Wrists Extend your arms and circle your wrists. Stretch your fingers, separating each one, and open and close the hands. This is essential for those who work on computers, to ensure that the arms, wrists and hands are relieved of the day's working tensions before dancing.

A short set-exercise routine each day will help to keep the body, muscles and blood ready for dancing and will also help relieve tension. The order in which you do the exercises is up to you; a good idea is to either start at the top of the body – neck, shoulders, hips, knees, ankles, feet, and toes – or start at the bottom – toes to neck. These very gentle exercises are not intended to be a full a work-out routine. Completing the exercise routine will also help you to understand balance and continuity of movement.

Walks Forward

Start with your weight on your right foot. Walk forward on to your left foot, then walk forward on to your right foot carefully 'brushing' it passed your left foot. Repeat for up to six walks forward.

Walks Backwards

Start with your weight on your right foot. Place your left foot back taking a small step. Extend your foot slightly beyond the body in order not to drop your weight backwards and lose your poise. Repeat for up to six walks backwards.

While you do this exercise, a little sing-song on this could be 'forward two three four, back two three four' using a musical count of one beat for each step. This can be danced solo or with a partner using the Double-hand hold.

THE BALLROOM

There is no set size or pattern for a ballroom. The room can be small or large, oblong, square or round. Corners can be a little disconcerting to a social dancer, so it is wise to think of the room as a circle and to travel in an anticlockwise direction. Check the directions of each dance carefully. The Waltz, for instance, will face the anticlockwise direction and the Social Foxtrot will travel towards the left because the man is facing the wall on the outside of the circle throughout the basic steps. There is no such problem for the Latin dances because most of them do not travel around the room. The exception is the Samba.

SOME DO'S AND DONT'S FOR THE BALLROOM

THE MAN

★ If you are dancing with a new partner, don't try your favourite variations or any complicated steps until you know that your partner is quite happy dancing with you.

★ Don't hold the lady too tight, give her room to move and breathe.

★ Do study carefully the direction of the dance around the ballroom.

★ Do listen carefully to the music before beginning the dance, to make sure that you are performing the correct dance.

★ Do start to dance by leading carefully, so that if you are going forward on the right foot you lead your lady to go back on her left foot.

★ Do escort your lady back to her seat after the dance. It is most disconcerting to be left in the middle of the floor at the end of a dance.

THE LADY

★ Don't refuse the offer of a dance without a good excuse. If you do refuse, do so graciously.

★ It is courteous to smile and make the man feel that you have enjoyed the dance.

★ If you are an unescorted female do make sure that you have done some practice of your

MUSIC

Music is a very important part of learning your first dances. Choose music that is the correct tempo for the dances you are going to do. With the tremendous selection of recordings available it is possible to obtain almost any good dance music from dance specialists (see list of stockists on page 128). Eventually, you will be able to improvise to almost any music.

Having chosen the piece of music you wish to dance to, listen to it, study it, and in your practice time fit your steps to it. Learn the number of beats and the rhythm of the music and then the steps will fit in more easily.

Many functions do not have a Master of Ceremonies, and many DJs do not actually say what dance is going to be played. It is expected that you would be able to recognise a Waltz, Cha Cha Cha, or a Rock 'n' Roll piece of music, and know what steps to use. Each dance has its own character, its own history, and its own music. By listening carefully and understanding the difference between various dances you will be able to recognise which dance to do. Learning about the history and the music of a dance is as essential as obtaining the correct foot positions.

own before going to a dance or a party.

★ Although it is the man's job to lead you, it is also your job to anticipate the next step.

★ Don't hold on to the man's right arm too tightly with your left hand.

★ Don't wear tight skirts. Make sure that you can move your legs freely.

★ Don't wear brand-new shoes.

★ Make sure to study the event you wish to attend, so that you can go with confidence and with the right attitude and the right clothes.

THE WALTZ

THE WALTZ IS BELIEVED TO HAVE STARTED in Austria as a folk dance in the 18th century, and made its way across Europe, through Germany and Bavaria, bringing with it the traditional music of those countries.

Possibly no other dance this century has caused so such controversy as the Waltz. When it first became popular in Britain in 1912 it was one of the first dances in which the man placed his arm around his partner and held her close. Although at that time there was no complete body contact between dancing partners, *The Times* newspaper felt that the Waltz was sufficiently risqué to warn its readers not to allow their daughters to take part in this 'voluptuous entwining of limbs'.

Earlier dances had been performed in circles, a style dating back to tribal rain dances and fertility rites. This circle dancing placed both the man and the lady on the same foot. In contrast, the Waltz is danced on opposite feet, with the lady mirroring the natural opposite steps to the man: if he uses his left foot, she uses her right. This change was quite a revolution in dance history.

One great problem that grew out of this new style of dancing was in the precise positioning of the feet. In earlier dances the feet were slightly turned out, which meant that a lady dancing with a partner might be hit by his out-turned heel. To put this right for the Waltz it was necessary for the dance masters of the day to find ways to straighten out the feet.

Today, the Waltz is one of the most popular dances in the ballroom, and is a certain feature at weddings and other celebrations. Nowadays, the music is less harsh, and the orchestrations softer and more sentimental than in the earlier German versions.

The Slow Waltz, now often referred to as the 'English' Waltz in recognition of the work of British dance teachers who helped to shape it as a competition dance, with complicated choreography and precise timing.

The Social Waltz, on the other hand, is quite easy to master. With only six basic steps forming the basis of the left and right turns to learn, anyone attending a social function will be able to join in the Waltz – and look at ease.

The slow tempo and repetitive rhythm of the Social Waltz make it a good dance for beginners to learn first. Blending the simple construction of the basic moves with the easy-to-hear beat of the music will come relatively easily and will help beginners to gain confidence quickly.

Bear in mind that the Waltz is likely to be played several times during an evening's dance programme, so it is well worth getting the basic steps right. Also, the Waltz is very often the last dance of the evening and is known as the 'Last Waltz'.

RIGHT-FOOT BASIC

STEP 1 *Count: 1 beat*

Man: Right foot forward – leading the lady to step back on her left foot

Lady: Left foot back

STEP 2
Count: 1 beat
Man: Left foot to side – leading the lady to step to right on her right foot
Lady: Right foot to side

STEP 3
Count: 1 beat
Man: Right foot closes to left foot – leading the Lady to close her left foot to her right foot
Lady: Left foot closes to right foot

LEFT-FOOT BASIC

STEP 1 *Count: 1 beat*

Man: Left foot forward leading the lady to step back on her right foot

Lady: Right foot back

STEP 2
Count: 1 beat
Man: Right foot to
side – leading the
lady to step to left
on her left foot
Lady: Left foot to
side

STEP 3
Count: 1 beat
Man: Left foot closes
to right foot –
leading the lady to
close her right foot to
her left foot
Lady: Right foot
closes to left foot

BOX TURN

1

STEP 1 *Count: 1 beat*

Man: Right foot forward – leading the Lady to step back on her left foot

Lady: Left foot back

STEP 2

Count: 1 beat

Man: Left foot to side
– leading the Lady to
step to side on her
right foot

Lady: Right foot to
side

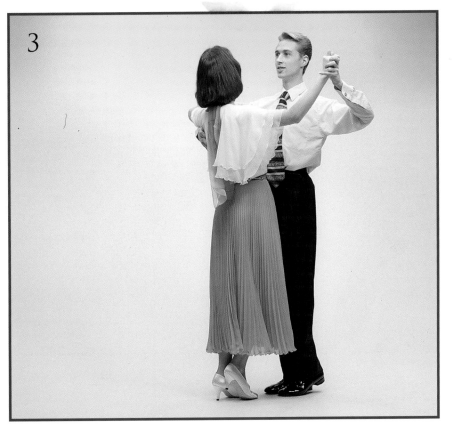

STEP 3

Count: 1 beat

Man: Right foot closes
to left foot – leading
the Lady to close her
left foot to her right
foot

Lady: Left foot closes
to right foot

STEP 4
Count: 1 beat
Man: Left foot back – leading the lady to step forward on her right foot
Lady: Right foot forward

STEP 5
Count: 1 beat
Man: Right foot to side – leading the Lady to step to side on her left foot
Lady: Left foot to side

6

STEP 6
Count: 1 beat
Man: Left foot closes to right foot – leading the Lady to close her right foot to her left foot
Lady: Right foot closes to left foot

SPECIAL TIPS

★ Social style hand hold. ▷

★ Practise hand hold. Always check that the hand holds are not too strong. ▽

★ Feet changing weight. ▷

When closing feet make sure to change the weight to the closing foot positively.

★ The Man should lead the Lady carefully. ◁

★ The Lady must be sensitive to the Man's lead. ▷

★ Check correct poise and head positions.

★ Listen carefully to the music, understand the beginning of each 'bar' of music. The drummer in the orchestra usually gives a strong 'one' count – it is on this strong beat that the first step is taken.

★ When the box turn has been mastered without a turn, gradually begin to turn to the right, keeping the box shape all the time but making a very gradual turn. Perform up to three 'boxes'. Always end facing the forward direction in which you will be travelling.

THE MAMBO

HE MAMBO IS PART OF THE CHA CHA Cha and Rumba family and is widely considered to be the 'mother' of the other Latin dances. The Cuban bandleader, Pérez Prado is credited with having started the Mambo in the 1940s. It is said that he took the rhythms of the dances performed by Cuban sugar-cane cutters out in the fields and developed them to form the Mambo beat.

By the middle of the 1950s the Mambo was the big dance craze in the clubs in Havana. According to some, the word 'mambo' comes from a dialect spoken in Cuba and has no real meaning. However, in Haitian Creole the word means 'voodoo princess', and perhaps that is the true origin of this spectacular dance.

Mambo is happy music, a combination of Latin and Jazz rhythms. Unfortunately, some Cuban and South American music can be quite difficult for dancers on this side of the Equator to relate to. In Britain it took a while for the Mambo to catch on in the dance clubs when it was first introduced. Because of the fast tempo of the music it can be difficult even for an experienced dancer, but there are now many recordings of Mambo music that are easy to hear – and easy to move the feet to.

The construction of the Mambo is almost identical to the Rumba except, because of the Mambo's faster tempo, the feet almost close on Step 3 instead of stepping to the side. The feeling is therefore of moving forward and backward. In the Rumba the step to the side enables the dancer to feel movement in the hips. In contrast the feeling in the Mambo is of movement in the knees and feet, so it is more natural for the dancer to almost close the feet on Step 3.

The Mambo also contains one particular feature to notice: there is one step in every bar where the dancer takes no step, but rests.

The Mambo has been groomed for competition and exhibition work but it is still a popular social dance in the many specialist Latin clubs that have sprung up around the country.

The steps for the Mambo are kept very small and rhythmic, with all the work being done flat on the balls of the feet. The way to master the speed and rhythm of the Mambo is to practice the first six steps of the basic movement before gradually introducing the figures.

The movements can appear rather staccato, and the correct stance for the Mambo is very upright – creating an almost regal appearance. It is worth remembering that it is better to have a short programme of perfect steps, and to be confident with just a few well-danced movements than to compromise the basic routine you have learnt trying to incorporate complicated formations. That will come later.

BASIC STEPS

Commence in close Latin hold, Man with weight on right foot.

Lady with weight on left foot.

STEP 1
Count: 1 beat – quick
Man: Left foot forward (Small Step) leading the Lady back on her right foot
Lady: Right foot back

STEP 2
Count: 1 beat – quick
Man: Replace weight back into right foot In-place – leading the Lady to replace weight into her left foot
Lady: Replace weight into left foot

STEP 3
Count: 2 beats – slow
Man: Left foot slightly back (half closes to right foot) – leading the Lady forward on her right foot
Lady: Right foot forward

STEP 4

Count: 1 beat – quick

Man: Right foot back (Small Steps) – leading the lady forward on her left foot

Lady: Left foot forward

STEP 5

Count: 1 beat – quick

Man: Replace weight forward into left foot – leading the Lady to replace weight into her right foot

Lady: Replace weight into right foot

STEP 6

Count: 2 beats – slow

Man: Right foot almost closes to left foot – leading the Lady to almost close her left foot to her right foot

Lady: Left foot almost closes to right foot

Repeat ad lib. Gradually turn to the left.

Have fun with the music when you dance the
Mambo.

DROP NEW YORK

To lead this figure release hold of the lady with
right hand on Step 6 of Basic movement.

STEP 1
Count: 1 beat – quick
Man: Left foot forward with strong 'bend' of left knee using 'drop' action – leading the lady to use drop action on her right foot forward
Lady: Right foot forward with strong 'drop' action

STEP 2
Count: 1 beat – quick
Man: Replace weight into right foot, In-place – leading the lady to replace weight into her left foot, In-place
Lady: replace weight into left foot, In-place

3

STEP 3

Count: 2 beats – slow
Man: left foot to side,
(Small step) – leading
the lady to step to
side on her right
foot. Regain normal
hold
Lady: Right foot to
side, (Small Step)

As man almost closes
left foot to right foot
on Step 3, he will
regain normal hold
and position with
partner then contin-
ue into Steps 4, 5
and 6 of basic move-
ment repeating the
'Drop New York' as
required.

Suggested routine:
Four sets of Basic
movement
Four sets of Drop
New York
Four sets of Back
Basic

SPECIAL TIPS

★ The knees should be very active and flexed. ◁

★ Hip action should be natural and not over-pronounced.

★ The basic movement can turn very quickly to the left using the backward half of the Basic to create the turn.

★ The hold is quite close.

★ Some pop music can be used, and often is in nightclubs and holiday resorts.

★ The music is very fast and therefore it is essential that the steps are kept small.

★ It is easy to improvise this dance and have fun once the steps have been mastered. ▷

THE FOXTROT

THE FOXTROT ORIGINATED IN THE UNITED States at the beginning of this century and rapidly grew in popularity during the Jazz era.

The Foxtrot features alternating long and short steps and its name is widely believed to be taken from these basic steps which supposedly match the movements of the fox. However, there are many other stories concerning the naming of the Foxtrot.

One, perhaps less plausible, version concerns a dancer called Harry Fox who appeared in a Vaudeville show in London around the time of the First World War. The show featured a sequence in which Mr Fox danced a series of trotting steps, with a few slows, between six or eight little trots. Some believe that Mr Fox's innovative steps marked the beginning of the modern Foxtrot.

The dance quickly became popular in British dance halls because it was easy to 'trot' around the dance floor to the fast beat of the music. However, the Foxtrot, in its original form, required a great deal of space on the dance floor and a high level of technical proficiency to cope with the demands of the up-tempo music. For the growing numbers of enthusiastic non-professional dancers in the nightclubs and dance halls of London the Foxtrot was not an easy dance to master.

Pressure from groups of social dancers in clubs around the country forced orchestras to develop different versions of the standard Foxtrot, and with help from prominent dance masters like Victor Sylvester the tempo of the music was reduced and the Slow Foxtrot was born.

The Slow or Social Foxtrot was to become one of the best loved dances in the ballroom repertoire. The dance has a feeling of lightness and is, above all, smooth and flowing, with the slows and quicks blending into one continuous movement.

In its true form the Foxtrot dancers must be completely relaxed and controlled in order to give the air of gliding across the floor. In its social form, however, the music has a heavier tempo which does not lend itself to rising on the toes, and although still a smooth movement, social dancers can achieve the feeling of floating across the dance floor that the professionals strive so hard to capture.

The basic movements of the Foxtrot are the Walk and the Three-Step. In its true form, as well as for the Slow Foxtrot, all the basic figures are based on these two movements.

Although purists agree that our understanding of modern ballroom dancing techniques has developed as a result of studying the complexities of the Foxtrot, it is still a dance for beginners to enjoy. Once the so-called 'connoisseurs' dance has been learned there will be no stopping the committed beginner.

SOCIAL FOXTROT – BASIC EIGHT STEPS

STEP 1
Count: 2 beats – slow
Man: Left foot forward – leading the Lady back on her right foot
Lady: Right foot back

STEP 2

Count: 2 beats – slow

Man: Right foot forward – leading the Lady to step back on her left foot

Lady: Left foot back

STEP 3

Count: 1 beat – quick

Man: Left foot to side – leading the Lady to step to side on her right foot

Lady: Right foot to the side

STEP 4

Count: 1 beat – quick

Man: Right foot closes to left foot – leading the Lady to close her left foot to her right foot

Lady: Left foot closes to right foot

STEP 5

Count: 2 beats – slow

Man: Left foot slightly back – leading the Lady forward on her right foot

Lady: Right foot forward

STEP 6

Count: 2 beats – slow
Man: Right foot back – leading the Lady to step forward on her left foot
Lady: Left foot forward

STEP 7

Count: 1 beat – quick
Man: Left foot to side – leading the Lady to step to side on her right foot
Lady: Right foot to side

STEP 8

Count: 1 beat – quick
Man: Right foot closes to left foot – leading the Lady to close her left foot to her right foot
Lady: Left foot closes to right foot

This figure is repeated until the music is completed, adding the Promenade variations as and if required.

Total musical count:
Slow Slow
Quick Quick
Slow Slow
Quick Quick

FOXTROT PROMENADE OR CONVERSATION PIECE

(A chance to talk to your partner)

PREPARATION: After closing feet on Step 8, turn Lady to a Promenade position (that means both facing in the same direction) ready to move forward.

STEP 1

Count: 2 beats – slow
Man: Left foot forward – leading the Lady forward on her right foot
Lady: Right foot forward

STEP 2

Count: 2 beats – slow
Man: Right foot forward – leading the Lady forward on her left foot
Lady: Left foot forward

STEP 3
Count: 1 beat – quick
Man: Left foot to side – leading the Lady to step to side on her right foot
Lady: Right foot to side

STEP 4
Count: 1 beat – quick
Man: Right foot closes to left foot – leading the Lady to close her left foot to her right foot
Lady: Left foot closes to right foot

This figure can be repeated.

SPECIAL TIPS

★ When dancing the Promenade, it is an opportunity to talk to your partner. ◁

★ The special lead is very important. The man uses his right hand to gently turn the Lady to face the same direction as himself. ▷

★The Lady must remember to return her head to normal dance position at the end of the Promenade steps. ▷

★ Turning to a Promenade position.◁

MUSIC TIPS

★ Listen carefully and identify the strong beats of the music.

★ Relax shoulders.

★ Move legs with soft knee action.

★ Try to maintain good balance at all times.

★ Make small, controlled steps.

★ Man to give careful leads to Lady.

★ Check direction around the room.

THE SAMBA

THE SAMBA IS UNMISTAKABLY THE DANCE of Brazil and its people. Every year in February towns and cities across Brazil grind to a halt and people fill the streets to celebrate the Carnival.

Samba and Carnival are inextricably linked: the exciting rhythms of the Samba, which can be seen and heard across the country during the festival, echo the mood of Carnival and capture the exuberant spirit of Latin culture.

Troupes of Samba dancers, all wearing flamboyant costumes, are carried through the streets on floats, each with a band playing a different tempo and creating a different mood. As much as spectators will admire the show, they will join in the fun, and dance in the street.

Outside Latin America, the Samba took a while to catch on. The expressive, exotic gestures of Samba were perhaps considered a little too earthy for a European audience. It was Carmen Miranda who brought Samba to North America and Europe and made the dance popular with a wider audience. She used tremendous panache and made the infectious rhythms of Samba accessible to a new generation and culture of dancers.

Later, the great American dancers Irene and Vernon Castle developed the dance into the ballroom style we know today.

It is interesting to note that its original choreography was for men only; it was considered improper and ungraceful for ladies to take part. Not until the Samba became a ballroom dance did it include steps and figures for couples dancing together.

Today, whilst Samba continues to be a national institution in Brazil, there are special Samba schools springing up across Britain, and once the unusual hip-tilt and bounce movements have been mastered, the Samba is a thrilling dance to learn.

It is written in 2/4 time and the rhythm is easy to follow, with one step for each beat. The feeling of embracing the rhythm so that your whole body reacts to the music and makes the Samba an invigorating dance to learn. Even the hand movements, which originate in early rituals of wafting aromatic herbs under the noses of the Samba dancers to intoxicate them with the fragrances are an important way into the mood of the Samba.

Outside Brazil people tend to think of the Samba as a one set dance. In fact there are many different versions, each with its own rhythm, tempo and mood. The steps for the social dancer are very easy, and the step pattern relates very closely to disco basic: simply side-close, side-close. This routine can be performed forwards and backwards, and turning to the right and to the left.

The basic steps described here will form a very exciting routine to be danced at any festival or party where Samba is played.

BASIC STEPS

Commence facing partner in normal hold position. Man weight on right foot, Lady weight on left foot, using bounce action in knees.

STARTING POSITION ▷

STEP 1

Count: 1 beat – slow
Man: Left foot to side – leading the Lady to step to side on her right foot
Lady: Right foot to side

STEP 2

Count: 1 beat – slow
Man: Right foot closes to left foot, with no change of weight – leading the Lady to close her left foot to her right foot
Lady: Left foot closes to right foot, with no change of weight

STEP 3

Count: 1 beat – slow
Man: Right foot to side – leading the Lady to step to side on her left foot
Lady: Left foot to side

STEP 4

Count: 1 beat – slow
Man: Left foot closes to right foot, with no change of weight – leading the Lady to close her right foot to her left foot
Lady: Right foot closes to left foot, with no change of weight

Repeat as required

WHISK OR CROSS

Commence in normal facing position. Man weight on right foot, Lady weight on left foot.

STEP 1

Count: 1 beat – slow

Man: Left foot to side – leading the Lady to step to side on her right foot

Lady: Right foot to side

STEP 2

Count: 1 beat – slow

Man: Place right foot behind left foot but do not change weight – use bounce action in knees – leading the Lady to place her left foot behind her right foot, without changing weight

Lady: Place left foot behind right foot, without changing weight

STEP 3

Count: 1 beat – slow

Man: Right foot to side – leading the Lady to step to side on her left foot

Lady: Left foot to side

STEP 4

Count: 1 beat – slow

Man: Place left foot behind right foot on ball of foot but do not change weight – leading the Lady to place her right foot behind her left foot and turn to Promenade position

Lady: Place right foot behind left foot, without changing weight

Suggested routine:
Four sets of Basic Side steps
Four sets of Whisks and as many Carnival Walks as required

CARNIVAL WALKS

A series of 'Walks' in Promenade position.

The 'Walks' follow the Whisks or Cross or after turning to Promenade position.

They can be danced solo turning on the spot, moving away from partner and moving towards partner.

Each 'Walk' has three very Small Steps and uses two beats of music, and is therefore counted 1 and 2.

The knees are flexed and the 'Walks' are danced with a Carnival atmosphere often using the arms and rolling the shoulders.

Feel the music in the knees with a soft bouncy action.

SPECIAL TIPS

This dance has many faces. It can be serious, a competition or exhibition dance, or it can be fun – a Carnival dance.

★ Bounce the knees softly – do not bend them. ▷

★ Use strong action on the ball of the foot to create a feeling of power into the floor. ◁

★ The music is very colourful with a constantly changing atmosphere, so it is important to understand this and to hear the music.

THE TANGO

*I*T IS GENERALLY ACCEPTED THAT THE Tango originated in the back streets of Argentina. for the people of the slums of Buenos Aires it was a gospel – some even say that it was treated as a religion! – more than just dance music.

Some of the distinctive clipped steps of the Tango came directly form the Argentinian cowboys who, after spending many months rounding up cattle out on the plains, came back into town in search of female company to take dancing in the local bars. Wearing their high boots, the cowboys' spurs would click as they danced, marking the staccato beats of the music.

The Tango reached Europe around 1900 and initially became very popular in France. When it was introduced to the smart set in England, Tango Teas and Dances soon sprang up all over London. For those who could afford the time and expense, it was possible to spend the entire afternoon dancing in the ball-rooms of London hotels, then nip home for a change of clothes to return in the evening to Tango some more.

George Grossmith is believed to have given the Tango its first boost in London in 1912 when he danced with Phyllis Dare in the musi-cal *The Sunshine Girl*, at the Gaiety Theatre. At that time aficionados of the Tango donned the flowing, full skirts that were fashionable amongst the Tango dancers of Latin America.

Before the First World War the Tango style was quite different to that taught by dancing instructors today. The music was slower, with a habanera rhythm, and there were no set steps. Dancers were encouraged in this free-style approach and it is said that no two teachers taught the Tango in the same style.

In October 1922 *The Dancing Times* spon-sored one of the first teachers' congresses to discuss the future of the Tango, new teaching styles, and how to make the dance more acces-sible. Over 300 teachers from across the country attended, and the results of the convention were far-reaching. The dance teachers were given a lot of material to develop the Tango and boost its popularity in their provincial ballrooms.

Today, the tempo of the Tango is about 30 bars per minute, and the style is to keep the feet straight and not turned out. The social Tango described here has only a few figures, since the original version features complex foot kicks and leg twists which are best studied after the basic steps and Promenade have been thoroughly learned.

To capture the dramatic moods and pos-tures of the Tango is surprisingly easy, and it is important to pay attention to the relative posi-tions of the body to create the atmosphere of tension and confrontation that makes the Tango such an exciting dance to learn.

BASIC PROMENADE

Commence in Promenade position, Man
weight on right foot, Lady weight on left foot.

STEP 1

Count: 2 beats – slow
Man: Left foot
forward in
Promenade position
– leading the Lady
forward on her right
foot in the same
direction as the Man.
Lady: Right foot
forward

STEP 2

Count: 1 beat – quick
Man: Right foot
forward in
Promenade position
– leading the Lady to
step forward on her
left foot
Lady: Left foot
forward

STEP 3

Count: 1 beat – quick

Man: Left foot to side – leading the lady to turn to face man in normal position on her right foot

Lady: Right foot to side, turning to face partner

STEP 4

Count: 2 beats – slow

Man: Right foot closes to left foot – leading the Lady to close her left foot to her right foot

Lady: Left foot closes to right foot

TANGO OVERSWAY

This will follow any movement when the feet have closed, for example, following the Promenade.

NOTE: This Tap Step is essential, it brings the man's left foot from the extended Oversway into a controlled position.

STEP 1

Count: 2 beats – slow

Man: Left foot to side, flexing knee – leading the Lady to side on her right foot, flexing her right knee, making a Tango Oversway position

Lady: Right foot to side, flexing right knee, creating Oversway

STEP 2

Count: 1 beat – quick

Man: Recover weight into right foot In-place – leading the Lady to recover weight into her left foot. This will automatically create a Tango Promenade position for Man and Lady

Lady: Recover weight on to left foot and finish in Promenade position

STEP 3 – TAP STEP

Count: 1 beat – quick

Man: Place left foot close to right foot without changing weight, lightly 'tapping' it on the floor in Promenade position

Lady: Place right foot close to left foot without changing weight, lightly 'tapping' it on the floor in Promenade position

SPECIAL TIPS

★ The Promenade is probably the most used figure in the Tango, and so we commence with it. However, it could be preceded with Tango 'walking steps', which are small, flat walks using 2 beats of music to each step.

★ This very special dance should be studied historically to understand its feeling.

★ The Tango has no rise and the steps are based on walking with a fairly flat action.

★ Listen carefully to Tango music to understand its very special rhythm.

★ It is important to study the recovery from the Oversway. ▷

★ The Man must work on the 'leads' to the Lady on the Promenade and Oversway. △

★ The Lady can develop leg 'flicks' and 'kicks' when she becomes proficient with the Basic actions. ▷

THE CHA CHA CHA

THE CHA CHA CHA WAS BORN IN THE dance clubs of Cuba, and is based on its Latin cousin, the Rumba. Like all Latin music the Cha Cha Cha is very percussive and sensuous, although it is less intimate than either the Rumba or the Samba.

Traditionally, Cuban dancers tended to dance in the open air, on a dust floor, so that their feet made a slight shuffling sound. This rhythm was picked up by the percussion players to produce a syncopation which became the Cha Cha Cha beat.

Today, the Cha Cha Cha is one of the most popular South American dances. When it was first introduced to this country it was danced in the ballrooms as a social dance. The beat was so infectious that the dancers just formed lines and all turned together or moved sideways in formation. It was great fun.

Many tunes based on the Cha Cha Cha rhythm were written in its early history, and many have survived. Cuban bandleader Pérez Prado's orchestra was one of the many to feature this now popular dance. There are many well-known songs, too, including Joe Loss's *Wheels Cha Cha Cha*, *Tea For Two*, and the song made famous by Shirley Bassey, *Never On A Sunday*. These songs are still played today and orchestras are continually introducing new Cha Cha Cha interpretations.

Most dance evenings will include at least one or two Cha Cha Chas in their programme, so it is an essential dance for the social dancer to have in their repertoire. The rhythm is easy to distinguish and you can very clearly hear the drummer beating out Cha-Cha-Cha-one-two, Cha-Cha-Cha-one-two.

Unlike the Mambo music which is complicated, the Cha Cha Cha music is usually played in a simple way. And as with the Samba and the Rumba, the movements of the Cha Cha Cha are light and continuous.

To get the real feeling of the Cha Cha Cha it is a good idea to rehearse the hips separately, just to get the feeling of the Cha Cha Cha rhythm. The movement of the feet should be very subtle: a few steps danced with feeling, and using the whole body will be much more enjoyable than having a large repertoire of steps where the brain has to keep working as well as the feet.

When learning the dance, try to work out the 'chassé to the left' and the 'chassé to the right'. Once this has been achieved the dance will come very easily since the only new formation to learn is the slight change in shape of the body in relation to your partner, and then the turns.

The actual step pattern never changes, so it is worth spending time and working hard on the feeling of 'Cha-Cha-Cha-Step-Step' before moving on to its many variations.

CHA CHA CHA TO THE RIGHT – EXERCISE

Count as 'Cha Cha Cha' when rehearsing – making a little sing song.

It is recommended that you rehearse these steps, three to the right and three to the left, many times, keeping the steps very small and always under the hips. Knees should be slightly flexed and hips very 'mobile'.

STARTING POSITION ▽

Commence, Man with weight on left foot, Lady with weight on right foot.

STEP 1

Count: ½ beat

Man: Right foot to the side – leading the Lady to step to the side on her left foot

Lady: Left foot to the side

STEP 2

Count: ½ beat

Man: Left foot closes towards right foot – leading the Lady to almost close her right foot to her left foot

Lady: Right foot almost closes to left foot

STEP 3

Count: 1 beat

Man: Right foot to side – leading the Lady to the side on her left foot

Lady: Left foot to side

CHA CHA CHA TO THE LEFT – EXERCISE

STEP 1

Count: ½ beat

Man: Left foot to side – leading the Lady to step to side on her right foot

Lady: Right foot to side

STEP 2

Count: ½ beat

Man: Right foot closes towards left foot – leading the Lady to close her left foot towards her right foot

Lady: Left foot closes towards right foot

STEP 3

Count: 1 beat

Man: Left foot to side – leading Lady to step to side on her right foot

Lady: Right foot to side

BASIC MOVEMENT IN-PLACE – TO THE RIGHT

STARTING POSITION

Commence, Man with weight on left foot. Lady with weight on right foot, preparing to dance Cha Cha Cha to the right.

STEP 1
Count: ½ beat
Man: Right foot to side –
leading the Lady to side on
her left foot
Lady: Left foot to side

STEP 2
Count: ½ beat
Man: Left foot closes
towards right foot –
leading the Lady to close
her right foot towards her
left foot
Lady: Right foot closes
towards left foot

STEP 3
Count: 1 beat
Man: Right foot to side –
leading the Lady to side on
her left foot
Lady: Left foot to side

MARK TIME IN PLACE

STEP 4

Count: 1 beat

Man: Left foot closes to right foot – leading the Lady to close her right foot to her left foot

Lady: Right foot closes to left foot

STEP 5

Count: 1 beat

Man: Replace weight into right foot, In-place, by slightly releasing the foot from the floor then replacing full weight into it. Replace – leading the Lady to replace weight into left foot as in Marking Time.

Lady: Replace weight into left foot slightly release it from floor and then replace full weight into left foot

BASIC MOVEMENT IN-PLACE –
TO THE LEFT

STEP 6
Count ½ beat
Man: Left foot to side – leading the Lady to side on her right foot
Lady: Right foot to side

STEP 7
Count: ½ beat
Man: Right foot closes towards left foot – leading the Lady to close her left foot towards her right foot
Lady: Left foot closes towards right foot

STEP 8
Count: 1 beat
Man: Left foot to side – leading the Lady to side on her right foot
Lady: Right foot to side

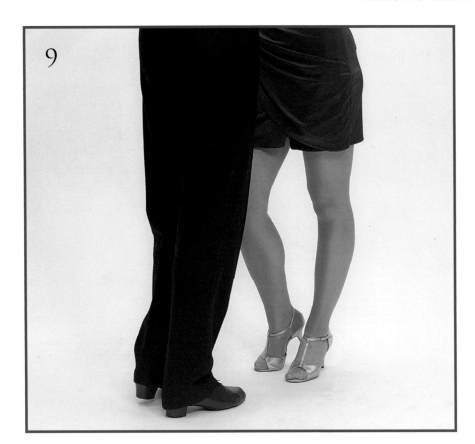

MARK TIME IN PLACE

STEP 9

Count: 1 beat
Man: Right foot closes to left foot – leading the Lady to close her left foot to her right foot
Lady: Left foot closes to right foot

STEP 10

Count: 1 beat
Man: Replace weight into left foot, In-place, by slightly releasing the foot from the floor and then replacing full weight into it. Replace – leading the Lady to replace weight into right foot (as in Marking Time)
Lady: Replace weight into right foot, slightly release it from floor and then replace full weight into right foot

FORWARD AND BACK BASIC
Commence with Cha Cha Cha to the right

STEP 1
Count: ½ beat
Man: Right foot to the side – leading the Lady to step to the side on her left foot
Lady: Left foot to the side

STEP 2
Count: ½ beat
Man: Left foot closes towards right foot – leading the Lady to almost close her right foot to her left foot
Lady: Right foot almost closes to left foot

STEP 3
Count: 1 beat
Man: Right foot to side leading the Lady to side on her left foot
Lady: Left foot to side

STEP 4

Count: 1 beat

Man: Left foot forward (Small Step) leading the Lady to step back on her right foot

Lady: Right foot back

STEP 5

Count: 1 beat

Man: Replace weight into right foot, In-place – leading the Lady to replace weight forward into her left foot

Lady: Replace weight forward into left foot

BACKWARD BASIC
Commence with Cha Cha Cha to the left

STEP 6
Count: ½ beat
Man: Left foot to side –
leading the Lady to side on her
right foot
Lady: Right foot to side

STEP 7
Count: ½ beat
Man: Right foot closes towards
left foot – leading the Lady to
close her left foot towards her
right foot
Lady: Left foot closes towards
right foot

STEP 8
Count: ½ beat
Man: Left foot to side – leading
the Lady to step to side on her
right foot
Lady: Right foot to side

STEP 9

Count: 1 beat

Man: Right foot back (Small Steps) – leading the Lady forward on her left foot

Lady: Left foot forward

STEP 10

Count: 1 beat

Man: Replace weight forward into left foot, In-place, by slightly releasing foot from floor and replacing weight into it – leading the Lady to replace weight into right foot

Lady: Replace weight into right foot

CHA CHA CHA NEW YORK - TO THE RIGHT

The Man will lead into this figure on Step 3 of the Cha Cha Cha to the right – releasing his right hand from the Lady with a slight turn to his right and the Lady's left which will prepare the foot position.

STARTING POSITION

Step 3 of Cha Cha Cha to the right as preparation step ▽

STEP 1
Count: 1 beat
Man: Left foot forward – leading the Lady forward on her right foot
(Man and Lady now in same direction using left hand hold only)
Lady: Right foot forward

STEP 2
Count: 1 beat
Man: Replace weight into right foot, In-place – leading the Lady to replace weight into left foot
Lady: Replace weight into left foot, In-place

CHA CHA CHA NEW YORK – TO THE LEFT

The Man will lead into this figure on Step 3 of the Cha Cha Cha to the left releasing his left hand from the Lady with a slight turn to his left and the Lady's right which will prepare the foot position.

STARTING POSITION

Step 3 of Cha Cha Cha to the Left as preparation step.

STEP 1

Count: 1 beat

Man: Making a slight turn on the left foot, right foot forward – leading the Lady forward onto her left foot (Man and Lady now face the same direction, right hand hold only)

Lady: Left foot forward

STEP 2

Count: 1 beat

Man: Replace weight into left foot, In-place – leading the Lady to replace weight into right foot

Lady: Replace weight into right foot, In-place

SPECIAL TIPS

Suggested routine:
Four sets of Basic In-place
Four sets of Forward and Back Basic
Four sets of New York
Repeat ad lib

★ The Cha Cha Cha Basic steps are consistent throughout the dance, so constantly rehearse the little sing song –

Cha Cha Cha Step Step
Cha Cha Cha Step Step

With this sing song in the brain the 'feel' will work more naturally.

★ Cha Cha Cha is a Latin dance and is therefore non-progressive. It is a dance almost In-place.

★ Remember, Small Steps.

★ The Forward and Back Basic can be turned gently to the left. ▽

★ Choose very distinctive Cha Cha Cha music.

★ Correct hand hold for the New York: Man's palm faces upwards and Lady's palm downwards. ▽

★ Its characteristic signs are a good use of hips, knees and feet. △

THE QUICKSTEP

HE FORERUNNERS OF THE QUICKSTEP were the Boston and the One-Step, which were popular dances in America at the peak of the Ragtime and Jazz era towards the end of the 19th century.

In the early 1920s the Charleston was a popular, if controversial, feature in American ballrooms. At the height of its popularity a now-legendary Charleston Ball was organised at the Royal Albert Hall. In its original form the Charleston was a wild dance and many enthusiastic, if ungraceful, amateurs were injured on the dance floor, giving rise to the slogan 'P.C.Q.' (Please Charleston Quietly).

When dance teachers began to realise the limitations of the Charleston – it was too fast and needed too much space – some of the moves were adopted into another dance of the day, the Quick-Time Foxtrot. This gradually evolved into what we now call the Quickstep.

The Quickstep rapidly became a standard ballroom dance and evolved, as its name suggests, to interpret the up-tempo music of the day with more sophisticated and smooth formations.

The dance went through many stages of development. Where the One-Step and the Boston were based on a forward step led with the heels followed by two or more forward steps on the balls of the feet, the Quickstep featured more complicated movements, based on Walks and Chassés. This gives the form of the Quickstep we dance today a much smoother feel than its early 'trotting' style.

In its social form the Quickstep has a basic pattern which is very similar to the social Foxtrot. With the Walks and Chassés there are always three steps, counted Quick-Quick-Slow, and all the basic formations revolve around these two movements together with the three-step foot pattern. Like the Waltz, diagonal patterns are used for the basic steps.

Once the basic Quickstep has been mastered it is possible to introduce many attractive variations. Because of the up-tempo feeling of the music it is essential to keep the steps small in order to keep time.

The dance moves quickly, so there is little time to think, which makes perfecting the basic steps essential.

BASIC EIGHT STEPS

STEP 1 *Count: 2 beats – slow*

Man: Left foot forward – leading the Lady to step back on her right foot

Lady: Right foot back

STEP 2

Count: 2 beats – slow
Man: Right foot forward – leading the Lady to step back on her left foot
Lady: Left foot back

STEP 3

Count: 1 beat – quick
Man: Left foot to the side – leading the Lady to step to the side on her right foot
Lady: Right foot to the side

STEP 4

Count: 1 beat – quick

Man: Right foot closes to left foot – leading the Lady to close her left foot to her right foot

Lady: Left foot closes to right foot

STEP 5

Count: 2 beats – slow

Man: Left foot slightly back – leading the Lady forward on her right foot

Lady: Right foot forward

STEP 6

Count: 2 beats – slow

Man: Right foot back – leading the Lady forward on her left foot

Lady: Left foot forward

STEP 7

Count: 1 beat – quick

Man: Left foot to the side – leading the Lady to step to the side on her right foot

Lady: Right foot to the side

STEP 8

Count: 1 beat – quick

Man: Right foot closes to left foot – leading the Lady to close left foot to right foot

Lady: Left foot closes to right foot

Note: Total musical count –
Slow Slow
Quick Quick
Slow Slow

PROMENADE OR CONVERSATION PIECE

PREPARATION

After closing feet on Step 8, turn Lady to a Promenade position (that means, both facing in the same direction) ready to move forward.

STEP 1

Count: 2 beats – slow

Man: Left foot forward – leading the Lady forward on her right foot

Lady: Right foot forward

STEP 2

Count: 2 beats – slow
Man: Right foot forward – leading the Lady forward on her left foot
Lady: Left foot forward

STEP 3

Count: 1 beat – quick
Man: Left foot to the side – leading the Lady to step to the side on her right foot
Lady: Right foot to the side

STEP 4

Count: 1 beat – quick
Man: Right foot closes to left foot – leading the Lady to close left foot to right foot
Lady: Left foot closes to right foot

NOTE: This figure can be repeated ad lib. The total musical count is Slow Slow, Quick Quick.

SPECIAL TIPS

★ Because of the speed of the music, steps must be kept small and positive. △

★ When dancing the Promenade the special lead is very important. The Man uses his right hand to gently turn the Lady to face the same direction as himself. ▽

★ As in all dances the Man should study the 'leads' and listen carefully to the music. △

★ The Lady must remember to return her head to normal dance position at the end of the Promenade steps. ▽

THE MERENGUE

HE MERENGUE IS AN OLD RITUAL DANCE and reflects the days of the African slave trade when slaves taken to South America had chains tied to their feet. As they walked and sang the chains rattled and provided percussive accompaniment. In its original form, the Merengue is not unlike a marching song.

The Merengue is the national dance of the Dominican Republic and many stories are told about its birth as a popular nightclub dance. Some say that it was first performed in the Dominican Republic by a lame general whose guests, not wishing to embarrass their host, dutifully imitated his moves as he limped with his bad left leg across the dance floor. This 'limp' step is still part of the Merengue, although it has since been refined.

The flat action of the Merengue is said to have been taken from the style which the local women had of walking whilst they carried water, washing and other heavy loads on their heads. The outstanding poise and balance needed to carry these loads, with the proud posture of the head, the dropped shoulder line and the straight back, are all attributes that the Merengue dancer tries to copy.

There is a lot of variety in Merengue music and the dance is now popular throughout the Caribbean and South America, as well as in specialist dance clubs in Britain. The tempo varies a great deal and one of the most popular is a slow *bolero*, breaking into the faster Merengue.

The beauty of the Merengue, and why is has become so popular with the modern generation, is that it is very adaptable. It is possible to dance to genuine Merengue music as well as to much of the current chart and pop music. It is also possible to dance alone when the mood takes you, or with a partner, and to make up the steps as you go along. Indeed the Merengue is often called 'the Thief' because its choreography has no real variations and, as the dance developed, all the 'new' shapes and patterns were actually stolen from other dances.

This is perhaps one of the easiest Latin dances to learn, since the foot pattern is simply marking time. The basic steps can be turned slightly to the left or slightly to the right, or with the feet apart and a very slight swing.

The Merengue is very much a lady's dance, with underarm turns and many variations. All changes of pattern are indicated by the man's hand movements and he must work hard to keep the loose hand-hold clear.

With all the possible variations and improvisations, the foot patterns always stay the same, so the Merengue is a great dance to try out your own choreography – and to have a lot of fun.

MERENGUE

This dance is based on a Marking Time movement, from left foot to right foot, giving equal beat value to each step. Use a strong ball-of-foot action but keep the feet fairly flat.

This dance is very much 'free style' and the emphasis is on rhythm. As the music is written in 2/4 timing, the steps are of equal musical value, and could perhaps be described as musical 'marching' using one step per foot per beat.

BASIC STEP

Count: 1 and 2

Man: Left foot – right foot (repeated)

Lady: Right foot – left foot (repeated)

The Basic Step can be danced in all directions: moving forward, moving backwards, turning to the right, turning to the left, moving sideways to the left and moving sideways to the right. Use these basic steps to change direction and make interesting shapes. Many of these Merengue movements are danced with the Double-hand Hold.

VARIATIONS

The following pictures show the patterns that can be danced using the basic steps. When dancing variation shapes the Man and Lady will continue Marking Time to the music, moving into the various shapes.

Lead the Lady by raising joined hands to turn to the left under raised arms.

Lady can also turn to her right under the raised arms. When leading the Lady to turn under the arm, the hand hold must be positive but soft.

Follow the pictures to make more interesting and exciting patterns.

It is fun to make up patterns and shapes, ensuring that the rhythm is marked at all times.

The dance is not meant to be technical and
should be great fun.

SPECIAL TIPS

★ The dance does not require a set technique.

★ It requires the dancers to listen to the music, feel the special phrases of intense rhythmic feeling. Be in a dancing mood and dance!

★ Be sure to use careful hand leads.

★ Invent moves and steps. ▽

★ It can be danced solo, or in a circle with friends at a party.

★ Keep steps small and rhythmic.

★ Use Marking Time action or soft 'marching' action' all the time.

★ The Merengue can be danced in sandals, or even bare feet.

ROCK/JIVE

By THE MIDDLE OF THE 1950s THE popularity of dance bands seemed to be on the wane and the youth of the day were listening to their favourite music on juke boxes. The younger generation had not lost their enthusiasm for dancing but they wanted a livelier style.

Jive/Rock, as its name suggests, is a blend of the fast-tempo Jive that was popular in America in the 1940s, and of Rock 'n' roll, which hit the dance clubs of America and Britain in the 1950s.

The forerunners of Rock/Jive have their own interesting history which is worth noting to fully understand the new dancing style.

It could be said that Jive is a watered-down version of the Lindy and the Jitterbug, both athletic dances that developed to cater for individuals who wanted the freedom of fast action, and to be able to improvise.

The Americans at that time were wearing shoes with 'sorbo' soles, like a sorbo bouncing ball, and were able to get a bounce action themselves, with increased spring in the exciting leaps and jumps of the Jitterbug.

This proved to be increasingly dangerous, with people getting injured in public ballrooms, and the Jitterbug was eventually banned except as a competition dance. The orchestras still played the music, but the dancers had to keep their feet on the ground. This scaled-down version of the Jitterbug was christened 'the Jive', bringing with it many stages of evolution. It was known by various names including the Lindy, West Coast Swing and American Swing. Each new name brought new movements, but the basic steps remained the same.

Musicians wanted to capitalise on this new young audience and when Bill Haley, famous for 'Rock Around The Clock', was discovered the young dancers in America went wild. Elvis Presley followed and the new Rock 'n' Roll music became the dance craze of the 1950s when it was introduced to Britain. What set Rock 'n' Roll apart from the Jive was that its style was meant for dancing in groups, rather than with a partner.

As the two dances merged the new style embraced all the old steps to produce a dance that was acceptable for all occasions. The new dance was refered to simply as Rock/Jive.

In the early days of circular skirts, a great emphasis was put on speed and how fast the girl could spin. This is not quite true today. Apart from competition dancing, just one or two spins are acceptable, and the emphasis now is much more on underarm turns, the change of hands behind the back, and dancing in a controlled way.

So much lovely music has come to us through Rock 'n' Roll and the Jitterbug, and no party is complete without a fun Rock/Jive session.

BASIC ROCK

STARTING POSITION
Man: Weight on right foot, feet slightly apart
Lady: Weight on left foot, feet slightly apart

STEP 1
Count: 2 beats – slow
Man: Place weight
into left foot, almost
In-place
Lady: Place weight
into right foot,
almost In-place
(with a slight rocking
action)

STEP 1A
Close-up of feet
position

STEP 2
Count: 2 beats – slow
Man: Place weight into right foot (Small Step)
Lady: Place weight into left foot (Small Step)
Perform step with a slight rocking action

STEP 2A
Close-up of feet position

STEP 3
Count: 1 beat – quick
Man: Left foot back
Lady: Right foot back
Perform step with a slight pull on joined hands

STEP 4
Count: 1 beat – quick
Man: Replace weight into right foot, In-place
Lady: Replace weight into left foot, In-place
Release tension in joined hands

FALL-AWAY

STEP 1
Count: 1 beat – quick
Man: Left foot back
in fall-away and
Promenade position
Lady: Right foot
back in fall-away
Promenade position

STEP 2
Count: 1 beat – quick
Man: Replace weight
forward into right
foot – leading Lady
to replace her weight
forward into her left
foot in Promenade
position
Lady: Replace weight
into left foot

UNDERARM HOLD
STEP 1

Count: 2 beats – slow

Man: Raising Man's left and Lady's right arm

Left foot forward (Small Step) – turning Lady to her right

Lady: Right foot forward starting to turn to right under raised arm

STEP 2

Count: 2 beats – slow

Man: Right foot In-place completing Lady's turn to her right, lowering joined hands, turning to face Lady

Lady: Left foot back completing turn to right. End facing partner

STEP 3

Count: 1 beat – quick

Man: Left foot back

Lady: Right foot back

STEP 4

Count: 1 beat – quick

Man: Replace weight into right foot, In-place, regain Double-hand Hold

Lady: Replace weight forward into left foot

SPECIAL TIPS

★ Exercise and loosen the knee joints and leg muscles. Rock/Jive works usually below the knee and uses a continuous 'down into the floor' action. △

★ Make sure to have pliable shoes and use strong ball-of-foot action.

★ Ladies – high heels are not comfortable to dance Rock/Jive in!

★ The music is sometimes very fast. Do not confuse Rock/Jive with Jive, which has a slightly different foot pattern and slower music.

★ Hands and arms should react in such a way that they could be described as a snake-like. They should seem to be without bones, completely pliable. ▷

★ Work on hand leads. This is the only communication with partner and when leading underarm turns, spins, etc. The 'hand' communication is of major importance for both Man and Lady. △

THE RUMBA

HE WORD 'RUMBA' IS REALLY A GENERIC term covering a variety of dance names including Afro Cuba Song, Dance Song, Guarjira Mambo Conga, and many others. It is believed that the original influences for the Rumba came in the 16th century when African salves were imported to Cuba.

The Rumba began as a fertility dance, echoing the courtship rituals of birds. Where many of the sensuous rhythms of Latin dances put the man in the dominant role, the Rumba places the emphasis on the lady, inviting her to make teasing gestures during the dance in order to attract the attentions of her partner.

Rumba has been described as the 'Queen of Latin American dances'. With its elegant poise, its classical style of steps when danced in the Social form, and its lovely rhythm, it was one of the first Latin dances to be fully accepted on this side of the Equator.

The main part of the development of today's Rumba took place in Cuba, where the original sources of the Spanish and African rumbas also evolved. The Spanish *Bolero*, with its slower tempo was also a strong influence, and to this day some musicians say that the Cuban Rumba is really no different to the Spanish *Bolero*.

Over time, the music has developed and in the Rumba we know today the tempos are much slower. Many people have tried to analyse Rumba music, and in its advanced form it can seem complicated. For the beginner this need not be the case. The basic steps are very simple; perfecting them. and getting the mood and feeling of the Rumba, can take years!

The music is written in 4/4 time and the dancer can either phrase the music into Quick-Quick-Slow, or Slow-Quick-Quick. The original Rumba was danced in a square pattern. The man will generally begin on his left foot, and gently turn to the left. There are variations which turn to the right, but the general feeling of the dance is a natural but gradual turn to the left.

The Rumba, being a Latin dance, is non-progressive and can be danced on the spot on a crowded dance floor. Because of this, movement is absorbed into the body to create a natural hip action and body rhythm.

For competitions the music gives the opportunity for elaborate choreography and it has become an interesting and very entertaining competitive dance. In its Social form, the Rumba just has a few basic steps and one or two underarm turns. The true feeling of the Rumba comes from correct use of the legs and hips and it is important to get the foot patter right first.

BASIC, IN-PLACE

Commence in normal Latin hold, Man's weight
on right foot, slightly to the side, and Lady's
weight on left foot to side.

STEP 1

Count: 1 beat – quick

Man: Left foot closes to right foot – leading the Lady to close her right foot to her left foot

Lady: Right foot closes to left foot

STEP 2

Count: 1 beat – quick

Man: Replace weight into right foot In-place – leading the Lady to replace weight into her left foot

Lady: Replace weight into left foot

STEP 3
Count: 2 beats – slow
Man: Left foot to side – leading the Lady to step to side on her right foot
Lady: Right foot to side

STEP 4
Count: 1 beat – quick
Man: Right foot closes to left foot – leading the Lady to close her left foot to her right foot
Lady: Left foot closes to right foot

STEP 5
Count: 1 beat – quick
Man: Replace weight into left foot, In-place – leading the Lady to replace weight into right foot
Lady: Replace weight into right foot

STEP 6
Count: 1 beat – quick
Man: Right foot to side leading Lady to step to side on her left foot
Lady: Left foot to side

Repeat and ad lib

FORWARD AND BACK BASIC

Commence with Man stepping to side on right foot – leading the Lady to side on her left foot.

STEP 1

Count: 1 beat – quick

Man: Left foot forward – leading the Lady to step back on her right foot

Lady: Right foot back

STEP 2

Count: 1 beat – quick

Man: Replace weight backwards into right foot, In-place – leading the Lady to replace weight forward into her left foot

Lady: Replace weight forward into left foot

STEP 3

Count: 2 beats – slow

Man: Left foot to side (Small Step) – leading the Lady to side on her right foot

Lady: Right foot to side

STEP 4

Count: 1 beat – quick

Man: Right foot back – leading the Lady forward on her left foot

Lady: Left foot forward

STEP 5

Count: 1 beat – quick

Man: Replace weight forward into left foot, In-place – leading the Lady to replace weight backwards into her right foot

Lady: Replace weight backwards into right foot

STEP 6

Count: 2 beats – slow

Man: Right foot to side (Small Step) – leading the Lady to step to side on her left foot

Lady: Left foot to side

Repeat ad lib. This figure can be turned gently to the left. Use Steps 4 and 5 to create turn.

NEW YORK

To lead the New York, release hold with right hand on Step 6 of Basic, In-place or Step 6 of Forward and Back Basic. This will 'open' the partnership on the man's right side (Lady's left side) preparing to both step forward in side-by-side position.

STEP 1

Count: 1 beat – quick

Man: With slight turn on right foot, left foot forward – leading the Lady forward on her right foot

Lady: Right foot forward

STEP 2

Count: 1 beat – quick

Man: Replace weight into right foot, In-place – leading the Lady to replace weight into her left foot

Lady: Replace weight into left foot

STEP 3

Count: 2 beats – slow

Man: Left foot to side turning to face partner and take Double-hand Hold – leading the Lady to step to side on her right foot to Man's left side

Lady: Right foot to side

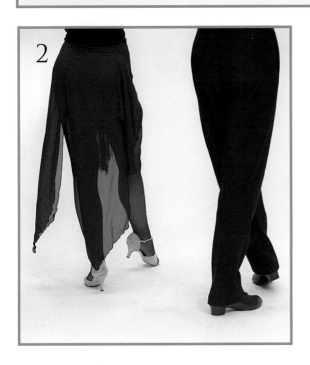

STEP 4

Count: 1 beat – quick

Man: With slight turn on right foot, right foot forward – leading the Lady forward on her left foot, having released hold with left hand

Lady: Left foot forward

STEP 5

Count: 1 beat – quick

Man: Replace weight into left foot In-place – leading the Lady to replace weight into her right foot

Lady: Replace weight into right foot

STEP 6

Count: 2 beats – slow

Man: Right foot to side (regain normal hold with partner) – leading the Lady to side on her left foot

Lady: Left foot to side, now facing partner

> **NOTE:**
>
> *Suggested practice routine:*
>
> Four Basic, In-place
> Four Forward and Back Basic
> Four New York to the right and left

SPECIAL TIPS

★ Work on hips to make them pliable and able to react to the music. Work on Small Steps. ▽

★ Practise Basic, In-place thoroughly before starting on next steps. ▽

★Keep good poise. Man to lead Lady carefully, Lady must be sensitive to Man's lead. ▽

★ Use Small Steps and lots of hip action.

★ Work on soft shoulders and expressive hands.

★ The rhythm is consistent – Quick Quick Slow – all the time. Make sure the 'feeling' of the Slow is a slightly longer count than the Quick, almost a pause.

★ The Slow count or slight pause is the opportunity to use the hip to roll it softly over the leg to give a Latin look.

★ Understand the lead from facing positions with partner, to side-by-side positions as in New York.

THE
WEDDING WALTZ

THE WEDDING WALTZ, IS SO CALLED
because it is danced at that most special of
events – the Wedding – and subsequently at
wedding anniversaries and such celebrations.

Wedding preparations often take a long
time, but do not leave learning how to Waltz
until the last minute. Work on it for as long
as possible so that opening the evening
party does not become a burden. You want
to be able to enjoy every second of this
wonderful occasion.

THE STEPS

The only two steps that are required are the
basic Waltz steps – right-foot basic and left-

MAIN POINTS FOR YOUR
WEDDING WALTZ

BEFORE THE DAY
★ Learn the steps (right-foot basic and left-
foot basic).
★ Practise picking up the train.
★ Take care when choosing the music.

ON THE DAY
★ Both the bride and groom should wear
comfortable and non-slip shoes.
★ Stand tall and proud and take plenty of
time, it is your moment.
★ Remember you will be photographed
while dancing.

---

foot basic (see pages 16-18). The bride
will usually wear a beautiful dress with a
long train so it is unwise to attempt more
complicated steps.

THE BRIDE
THE DRESS

Remember that your beautiful dress has been
designed for you to walk in a forward direction, showing the back of the dress. When you
are dancing you will move mostly backwards –
this needs consideration before the great day.

★ Take time to practise moving in your dress.
Try stepping backwards. This is very important, particularly if you are not used to wearing
a long dress. The danger is that the shoe heel
can catch in the hem so the dress needs to
move a little to allow the feet to move back.
★ If the dress has a train that is not removable
make sure a loop is sewn in so that you can
pick up the train with your left hand before
starting to dance.

THE SHOES

New shoes are not a good idea for dancing so,
if possible, wear your shoes 'in' around the
house before your wedding day so that your
feet do not become sore and tired. Normal
court-type shoes are good to dance in but
heelless shoes, so often chosen by brides, are
very difficult to dance in. They are designed
for you to move forward in but not backwards.
You could take a step backwards and leave
the shoe behind.

★ A wise precaution is to have a spare pair of more comfortable shoes near to hand for the evening festivities so that your feet are comfortable, not only for dancing but for the inevitable walking around greeting guests.

★ Make sure that the soles of your shoes are not likely to slip.

THE GROOM

★ Be sure to allow the bride to be 'comfortable' before starting the Wedding Waltz. It is your day, your moment, so do not hurry and possibly spoil that special feeling.

★ Remember that the cameras are recording this part of the occasion, so stand tall and proud – do not lean over your bride; allow her freedom to also stand tall and show off her beautiful dress.

★ Take care with your right-hand hold as she may have her 'train' in her left hand. Place your right hand gently around her waist.

★ Make sure you indicate which foot you will use. It is not wise to spring surprises!

★ Try to direct your steps in an anticlockwise small circle so that you cover the whole floor in a subtle way! All the guests love to have a photograph of this very special Waltz.

THE MUSIC

The correct choice of music is very important as it is the tune that will remain in your memory for years to come. Try to choose a tune that is a favourite and is played in Waltz tempo, making it easier to keep to the rhythm of the beat. The trap that many fall into is choosing a favourite tune, then discovering that it is not in Waltz tempo. With careful research, a wonderful tune in Waltz tempo can be found.

119

THE
BASIC HOLDS

N THE DANCE FLOOR, THERE IS NOT TIME to go through the set positions of the hold before starting each dance, so the basic holds must be practised beforehand, perhaps in front of a mirror. In the beginning the holds can feel a little stilted and unnatural but eventually they will become easy and feel quite natural.

Stand facing each other with your feet almost together and keep your poise and balance correct.

The man raises his right arm from the elbow and places it just below the lady's left shoulder blade.

The lady places her left hand at the top of the man's right arm.

The man raises his left arm, again from the elbow, keeping it on his side of the partnership. The man allows the palm of his left hand to face the lady.

The lady will then place her right hand over the palm of the man's left hand. You should hold each other's hands very gently.

★ There should not be any tension in the lady's or the man's left arm.

★ Check very carefully that the man is not actually pushing the lady back over her heels. In order to retain her balance she will anchor herself to the floor, so she will find it extremely difficult to move.

★ A good exercise is to practise your position without your partner. Stand with your arms folded in the right position and check your poise and balance.

These photographs show the basic holds. Study them carefully so that you know the differences.

1 *Double-hand practise hold.*
2 *Lady's wide hold for ballroom dancing.*
3 *Man's wide hold for ballroom dancing.*
4 *Close hold, social, for ballroom dancing.*
5 *Close hold for the Tango.*
6 *Forward hold for the Tango.*
7 *Promenade position with both partners facing the direction in which they are travelling.*

WHAT TO WEAR

WHAT CLOTHES TO WEAR TO DANCE IN depends on the type of function you will be attending, be it a dinner dance, party or a holiday dance. A general tip is to wear comfortable, but smart and elegant clothes to go dancing – a holiday disco is usually very casual. A few general rules will cover everything.

LADIES

★ Try not to have sleeves that are large and dangle. They make it difficult for the man to put his right arm around you.

★ Wearing an angora jumper or anything where the threads can be transferred to the man's suit is not a good idea at all!

★ If you are wearing a long evening dress always look in the mirror and check that when you step backwards you are not going to step on to the skirt of the dress, which may then either tear the dress or result in a fall.

MEN

★ If you are attending a dinner dance, always check if a dinner jacket and formal wear is required.

★ Many clubs and discos do not allow a man in without a tie.

SHOES

The correct footwear for dancing is even more important than the clothes. The wrong shoe makes it difficult to dance well.

Michael Free, the founder of Supadance International, spent a lifetime researching and making shoes for dancers, from beginners to the top professionals. All his shoes are designed in collaboration with the top dancers to make sure that they fit correctly and are comfortable.

All dance shoes must fit perfectly and not be too new and slippery. Wear them in around the house before venturing on to a dance floor. Ladies, avoid sling-back heels as they do not give enough support and are not good for dancing backwards and avoid heels that are too high.

The following shoes are a selection recommended for the various types of dancing.

1 *Junior girls' shoe*
2 *Ladies' practice shoe*
3 *Men's international dance shoe*
4 *Ladies' Latin shoe*
5 *Ladies' Ballroom shoe*

PROFILE:
JOHN BYRNES & JANE LYTTLETON

OUR DANCING CAREER HAS GIVEN US INNUmerable opportunities to travel extensively around the world, making new friends and experiencing different cultures, and to 'work' doing something we love, as well as living life to the full.

At the age of eight, I (John) was involved in football, judo and Boy Scouts, when my mother decided I should learn to dance. I am not sure if it was because of my high energy levels or if it was to keep me out of mischief or to teach me etiquette. I did my medal examinations and started competitive dancing, travelling throughout Australasia. As an amateur, I won the Australian Championship, and was a finalist at the World 10 Dance Championship, and semi-finalist at the World Modern Championship in Germany. It was at this time that I decided to move to England because I wanted to be the best in the world.

Jane began dancing at the age of seven in Stoke-on-Trent, England. She achieved high honours in her medal examinations and won the Juvenile Mixed Doubles at the Open British. As a junior she travelled the world making all the major championship finals. In the Amateur Latin American Championships she made the Closed British final and the semi-finals of all the major championships.

In 1986 we teamed up and have been together ever since. We won the European 10 Dance Championship in Denmark, our first championship representing England. We won the Closed British American Championship twice, and were regular finalists in all major championships in the world.

We have appeared on television and radio shows around the world including the BBC's *Strictly Come Dancing* in 2004, in movies such as *Evita*, and have performed at Elton John's birthday party.

In 2001 we were married and in January 2004 we had a baby boy. We retired from competative dancing in 2002 but will continue to do our dance cabaret. We teach around the world and currently run a dance school in Beckenham, Kent.

No matter what your level of dancing, the beginner or competitor, to learn to dance teaches you important social skills and self esteem, gives you confidence and a sense of achievement that is unequivocal euphoria!

All the best with your dancing.

John & Jane

RECENT CHAMPIONSHIPS:
United Kingdom Closed Latin American: *2002*
British National S.American Showdance: *2000*

PROFILE:
CHRISTOPHER HAWKINS & HAZEL NEWBERRY

*H*AZEL AND I HAVE BEEN DANCING together for over ten years now. In that time we have been more successful than we could have dared to imagine when we first took hold for a trial at the Grafton Ballroom in Dulwich.

Hazel's first thought when we met must have been that I was a very rude young man! I was so eager to get on with the trial that, after some hasty introductions, I threw her in at the deep end and immediately danced my normal Foxtrot choreography twice around the floor. Hazel did well to follow my every move, especially when I realised that I had not even told her which dances we were going to do!

Three weeks later, we had already danced in our first competition and we were training hard in preparation for our first big win, the Open British Under 21 Years Championships.

But our long term goal was to become the best dancers in the World, and little did we know our dream was soon to be realised. In 1997, we won a Gold medal at the World Games held in Finland. This was the first time that dancesport had been part of a major athletic event, so we were excited at the opportunity to demonstrate that we were not just good dancers, but also good athletes.

Later that year we won the World Amateur Ballroom Championships and then turned Professional. In the ensuing years, we worked our way up the Professional ranks, achieving both National and International success. We became World Professional Champions in 2002, a title we have retained ever since.

Alongside our competition successes, we have enjoyed a full schedule of showtime performances, and have been much in demand for teaching, lecturing and demonstrating all over the world. We have made several videos, frequent TV appearances and entertained royalty and media stars.

Our main objective has always been to make dancesport accessible to a wider audience, and we consider ourselves fortunate to be able to do just this.

Christopher & Hazel

RECENT CHAMPIONSHIPS:
World Professional Modern: *2004, 2003, 2002*
United Kingdom Professional: *2004, 2003*
Open British Professional: *2004, 2003*
Open Italian Professional: *2004*
International Professional: *2003, 2002*
European Professional Modern: *2003*
Open Asian Professional: *2003, 2002*
Open United States Dancesport: *2002*

GLOSSARY OF TERMS

ad lib: Repeat the steps or figures as required.

Beat: The note of the music used for the step. Sometimes two beats are used for one step, in which case the music is said to have a slow beat. Sometimes one beat is used for one step, in which case it is known as having a quick beat.

Choreography: The composition or arrangement of a dance. In social dancing the steps of three, or four figures in each dance are all that is really necessary. A dance loaded with variations often proves to be antisocial in a crowd and an unnecessary burden on the dancer.

Close Hold: The two bodies are close together. This is the normal hold for most ballroom dances.

Competition dancing: This is an extravagant style of dance, specially choreographed and specially dressed. It is designed for couples who wish to have their standard of dancing assessed by adjudicators.

Direction: This mostly applies to ballroom dances which are described as the 'moving' dances must have correct directions around the ballroom or club.

Following: It is the role of the Lady to follow the man. Learning to follow and be led is as much a part of the art of dancing as learning the steps. The Lady must develop a sensitivity to the Man's lead and at no time attempt to take on the role of leader.

In-place: Steps with this instruction indicate that you should not travel backwards, forwards or sideways. This can also be described as marking time.

Leading: The role of the Man is to lead the partnership. Leading requires an understanding of every step and change of step for each dance. He must be able to transmit his intentions to his partner and he must also understand the music in order to indicate on which beat of music to start each dance.

Musical count: The time taken for each step when dancing to music. A slow count is when a step takes two beats and a quick count is when a step takes one beat (see **Beat**). Sometimes the reference will be numerical but in the 'Cha Cha Cha' the actual words Cha Cha Cha are used in the muscial count!

Open Hold: A hold in which the two bodies are slightly apart, as in most Latin dances.

Practice Hold: The hold with which to practise steps at first before taking a close or open hold. It is known as the Double-hand Hold.

Preparation step: The step that precedes a new movement. It is also a term used for the starting foot, before commencing to dance any step.

Promenade: The position in which both the lady and man are facing in the same direction and will dance in that direction, in contrast to the normal dance position which has them facing each other.

Side-by-side: A dance position in which both dancers are facing the same way ready to dance in that direction.

Social: The type of dances used for social occasions such as weddings, holidays and parties. The dances should be simple and smart in style, and the dancers should use small steps and keep an awareness of other dancers.

WHY JOIN A DANCING SCHOOL?

You will learn all the basic steps required to make you proficient by using this book at home. It is a convenient way in which to overcome any natural shyness about being 'left-footed' in public. There is, however, much to be said for also joining your local dancing school, especially if you want to advance and improve your technique.

A good dancing school should be able to teach you how to dance, giving encouragement and confidence, as well as providing social events in which you can participate. Many people want to dance as a way to meet people of all ages who have a similar interest. Dancing schools are not just for those who want to become competitive dancers.

Some areas have more than one to choose from, so talk to your friends and visit them to see for yourself which one you think is most suitable for your requirements. Here are some of the things to look out for and some of the questions you should ask.

Where is it?

A dance school needs to be convenient either to your home or place of work. Make sure that there are car parking facilities, or it is close to public transport. Will you be safe at night?

Do the school hours suit you?

Is the school open at times convenient to you and offering the classes you want at these times? Do they have facilities for children if required?

What fees are payable?

Many schools have a membership fee, which gives you access to all facilities. Some will offer a price for a series of classes or private lessons. Check if these need to be paid for in advance or if they can be paid for in installments.

Does the school feel comfortable?

When looking around a school consider whether you would feel welcome and comfortable being there? Ask about social functions such as Tea Dances and Social Dance evenings.

Are the classes crowded?

Check out how many people are usually in a general class. Also, ask what facilities are available for individual classes.

What are the classes like?

A good school will offer a variety of classes for all levels, ages, and abilities, as well as classes for children.

What are the general facilities like?

It is a good idea to look at the changing rooms – are they clean and tidy with a good standard of hygiene? Are the reception areas clean and welcoming with friendly staff who are not intimidating to the newcomer?

What are the refreshment areas like?

There should be clean, comfortable bar or refreshment areas where it is pleasant to meet new and old friends. The food on offer should be fresh and healthy, the sort of thing you would want to eat regularly.

Having found all the things you need you will be able to put into practice with other people all the steps you have learnt from this book.

USEFUL CONTACTS & INFORMATION

ALL DANCE INFORMATION
British Dance Council
240 Merton Road
South Wimbledon
London SW19 1EQ. UK
Tel: + 44 [0]20 8545 0085
Fax: + 44 [0]20 8545 0225
Email: secretary@british-dance-council.org

Ballroom Dancers Federation
Administrative Office
8 Hazelwood Road
Cudham
Sevenoaks
Kent TN14 7QU. UK
Tel: + 44 [0]1689 855 143

World Rock'n'Roll Confederation
Wolfgang Steuer
Schutzenstrasse 8
D-80335 Munchan. Germany
Tel: + 49 89 59 67 05
Email: wolfgang.steuer@tanz.de
*The above will be able to give advice on
dance classes and general dance information.*

DANCE ACCESSORIES
DanceSport International Ltd
[Trading as Hearn & Spencer Ltd]
The Courtyard
Aurelia Road
Croydon CR0 3BF. UK
Tel: + 44 [0]20 8664 8188
Fax: + 44 [0]20 8664 8288
*DanceSport sell dance shoes for both compe-
tition and social dancing, accessories, and
have a large range of dance videos, dance
music cassettes CD's and books.*

DANCE SHOES
Supadance International Ltd
159 Queen's Road
Buckhurst Hill
Essex 1G9 5BA. UK
Tel: + 44 [0]20 8505 8888

Julienne
163 High Street
Beckenham
Kent BR3 1AE. UK
Tel: + 44 [0]20 8650 5796

Julienne
820 Wickham Road
Croydon CR0 8EB. UK
Tel: +44 [0]20 8777 3750

Freed of London
94 St Martins Lane
London WC2N. UK
Tel: + 44 [0]20 7240 0432
Fax: + 44 [0]20 7240 3061
Email: shop@freed.co.uk
*The above shoe manufacturers specialise in
most types of dance shoes.*

CLOTHES
Chrisanne
14 Locks Lane
Mitcham
Surrey CR4 2JX. UK
Tel: + 44 [0]208 640 5921
Fax: + 44 [0]208 640 2106
Boutique Tel/Fax: + 44 [0]208 770 1827

Choice London Ltd
Old Book House
342-44 London Road
Mitcham
Surrey CR4 3ND. UK
Tel: + 44 [0]20 8715 9200
Fax: + 44 [0]20 8715 9222
Email: sales@choicelondon.net

Faberge Fabrique Ltd
1370c London Road
Norbury
London SW16 4DE. UK
Tel: + 44 [0]20 8679 6547
Fax: + 44 [0]20 8764 8243
Email: info@dance-shop.com

MUSIC
Ross Mitchell
1 Queen's Road
Fleet
Hampshire GU13 9LA. UK
Tel: + 44 [0]1252 629740
Fax: + 44 [0]1252 811788

Tema International
151 Nork Way
Banstead
Surrey SM7 1HR. UK
Tel: + 44 [0]1737 219 607
Fax: + 44 [0]1737 219 609

C&D Dance Records
145 Chestnut Avenue
Eastleigh
Hants SO50 5BB
Tel: + 44 [0]2380 614476
Also see DanceSport International Ltd